THE
BORIS VALLEJO
PORTFOLIO

This edition published in Great Britain in 2000
by Paper Tiger
An imprint of Collins & Brown
London House, Great Eastern Wharf
Parkgate Road, London SW11 4NQ
www.papertiger.co.uk

Distributed in the United States and Canada by Sterling Publishing Co,
387 Park Avenue South, New York,
NY 10016, USA

First published by Dragon's World in 1994

9 8 7 6 5 4 3 2 1

British Library Cataloguing-in-Publication Data:
A catalogue record for this book is available from the British Library.

ISBN 1 85585 792 8

Editor: Fiona Trent
Art Director: John Strange
Jacket design: Claire Graham

Printed and bound in Italy by Eurolitho

LIST OF PLATES

One of the impressive aspects of Boris Vallejo's work is the length to which he will go to achieve the intense realism characteristic of his paintings. Many artists would be content with the standard of some of his preparatory drawings that he produces straight from the imagination, particularly those finished with coloured inks; they stand comparison with the very best comic book art, but they are not complete in Vallejo's eyes. Often, the final painting is not markedly different in overall composition to the draft sketches, but it does differ in its overwhelming sense of realism; one almost feels able to step into the finished painting. The draft is a powerful drawing, the completed work is like a living slice of some dream or nightmare.

Heroic fantasy is to Vallejo what water is to the proverbial fish and it comes as no surprise that his talents have been in demand for illustrating such characters as Conan the Barbarian, Tarzan and Doc Savage. But, curiously, he tried several other fields of professional illustration before realizing that heroic fantasy was his natural artistic home, being as it is the perfect vehicle for exercising his fascination with human and animal physique – the human side arising from an abiding interest in body building. Human figures dominate his pictures, might-muscled men and voluptuous women who, in the tradition of the genre, are almost always scantily clad.

Painting or drawing from life lies at the heart of Vallejo's facility with human figures. For practical reasons he usually works from photographs of models rather than having them pose in the flesh, but to compensate for the inevitable limitations of this he draws on a long experience of straight life drawing. And, in any case, the model or photograph is only a starting point. This is, after all, fantasy painting and not a documentation of mundane reality. In the process of transferring a drawing or photograph on to board for the final painting many conscious and unconscious modifications of the image take place, leading the painted image to look far more dramatic than its original reference. Vallejo's figures are rooted in reality but he has long since passed the stage of having to copy nature slavishly.

Proof of this is that his totally mythical creatures carry the same stamp of authority as the human figures. Obviously imagination has a much freer rein with these creatures, but one of the reasons they convince is that they are derived from careful observation of the natural world. Often they contain human elements and have been improvised from combinations of human and animal photographs but, as with human figures, the photographs are only a starting point. In theory anyone could cut up a random assortment of animal pictures and come up with a monster, but the chances of it being convincing are slim.

A firm grasp of anatomy and the artistic ability to blend the elements smoothly are required and even these skills are not necessarily enough to do the trick. With imaginary creatures it is not just the eye that needs to be convinced, the choice of elements in a hybrid creature is also vital. That part of the imagination to which fantasy appeals, the mystic bit that feeds our dreams, has its own ideas about what does and does not work. No matter how cleverly they are painted, some monsters just look silly, while others leap from their two dimensional cage and print themselves

indelibly on our subconscious. Knowing the difference between the two is what makes a fantasy artist.

It hardly needs to be said that what Boris Vallejo does, he does supremely well. If your taste is for heroic fantasy, he is your man. On occasion the erotic aspect of this realm, which is never far below the surface, has received his full attention as demonstrated by the book *Mirage* with accompanying poems by his wife Doris. Vallejo ends the introduction to *Mirage* with a comment that sheds interesting light on his attitude towards the theme: 'When I see a beautiful woman in the street I enjoy looking at her. Do I start imagining how it would feel to touch her? What it would be like to make love to her? Not at all, though some of that may find expression in a painting sometime. Still, at the moment, I just enjoy what I see.'

At another point, describing his feeling about one of his paintings of a female clad only in high black boots and a leather jacket standing before a monster, he says: 'I love that leather jacket: the folds, the shine, – I can actually feel it. Everything is right there. And I love the head of that monster. I really enjoy his expression, his ugliness as well as the little details of the veins and the different colours. I can almost hear the screech of that monster. And this, to me, is exciting. I can't plan these things ahead of time. Much of my painting is instinctive. Things happen as I work. As I worked on the monster, on his open mouth, I began, as I said, almost to hear him. As I was doing the veins in his head I could feel the texture of the skin stretched over them. But I had none of that in mind when I began. It wasn't the result of any cerebral plotting.... What I consciously aim for in painting is, more than anything else, to create a visual impact. And, to me, figure is the ultimate test; to be able to hold the viewer in thrall without relying on excessive detail or on a whole crowd scene – this is excellence in painting.'

The world divides between people who are visual and those who are not. That is, many people recognize that they are lucky not to be blind, but only use sight in a mechanical way, as a means to other ends. It is not a source of pleasure and fulfilment in itself as perhaps music, ideas, feelings or physical sensation is to them. But, you do not have to be an artist to have a highly developed visual sense, although artists are probably more aware than most other visual people of at times speaking a different language to those around them. Many people may appreciate the effects of what they produce, this is the age of film and television after all, but far fewer understand the means by which it is achieved. Or even want to.

Boris Vallejo is rare among artists in being almost as comfortable expressing himself in words as in images and anyone curious to know more about his motivations and, in particular, his methods of achieving the effects he does, is recommended to search out his other books. But for those who wish simply to enjoy his paintings, or enjoy them on a larger scale than previously published, this portfolio contains a wonderful sampling of what he has achieved to date.

1
THE TORCH

2
THE MAGNIFICENT

3
EGYPTIAN WARRIOR

4
CAPRICORN, THE GOAT

5
SAGITTARIUS, THE ARCHER

6
NUBIAN WARRIOR

7
THE LAVALITE WORLD

8
HAESEL THE SLAVE

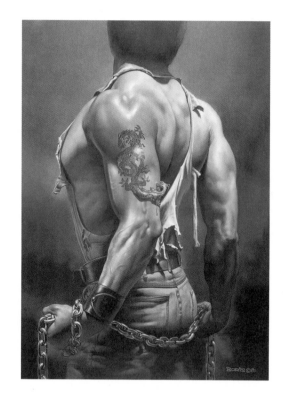

9

TATTOO

BORIS©81

10
JADE MANIKIN

11
Alpnu

12
DRAGON'S KNIGHT

13
QUEEN OF THE AMAZONS

14
DUMBELL

15
DISCUS THROWER

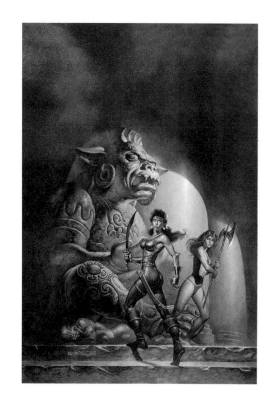

16
MOTHER AND DAUGHTER

17
AGAINST THE ODDS

18
GEMINI, THE TWINS

19

SECRETS OF SYNCHRONICITY

20
SCARLET MENACE

21
TWO-HEADED BEAST

22
HEAVY METAL

23
THE BRIDE

24
MAYAN SERPENT

25
KNIGHT ON WHEELS

26
THE VICTORIOUS

27
ATLAS

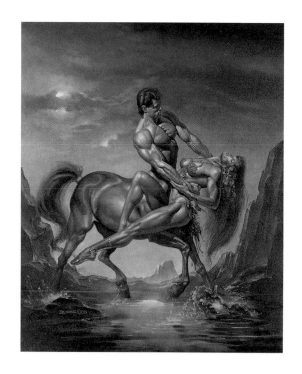

28
DEIANEIRA AND NESSUS